ON THE BRINK...

IF ONLY WE had ten thousand people with the passion and energy of Pat Arrowsmith — the British Isles would be swept clean of nuclear weapons and the troops would be back from Ireland overnight.* And then our ten thousand Pats wouldn't take a holiday — they'd be off in the morning, five thousand to Washington, five thousand to Moscow to sort those villains out with some good humane common sense.

It goes without saying that Pat is brave — there is plenty to fear in the barbaric prisons to which she's sent time after time for opposing mass murder. It is more important to say that Pat is right. England is still asleep. England must be woken. These may well be the last days of the planet we love. If we do love this planet. And if we do love this planet, now's the time to show it.

Pat shows her love through her life and through her poetry. You can [illegible] two of course. I've heard people say: "I'd like [illegible] political poems." The only answer is: "Then live a political life".

Wilfred Owen explained that poets must warn. Pat has continually warned us of the dangers we're in and the new dangers we're creating. See her poem about a rock pool or her vision of a "ruby-gleam fairground" and you'll understand that she's fully aware of the beauties of the world. And in the same poems she emphasises how the human race threatens itself and Nature too.

We need Pat and we need her poems. Her words are angry and clear and urgent. They will help to change the world for the better. Use them.

Adrian Mitchell

* See page 22.

Poems by Pat Arrowsmith

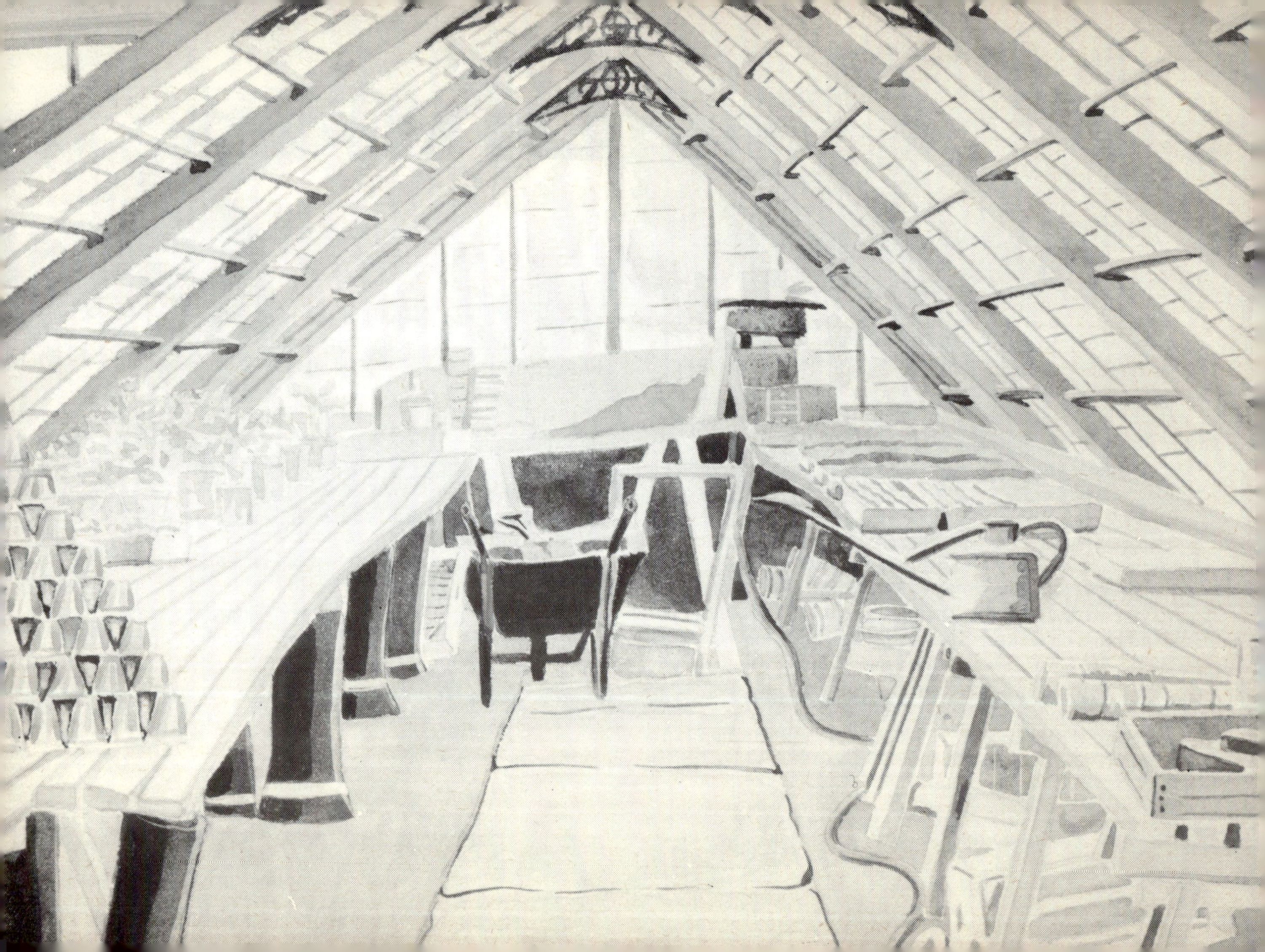

Greenhouse

Line upon line of cuttings,
tangle of tendrils and foliage vibrant
with sap, lit here and there by
geranium flame.

Clusters of fern absorbing the
soil's wetness,
breathing out an earthy musk into
the warmed air.

Flower pots crowded into
glowing ranks stretch
away down the staging seemingly
for ever.

The greenhouse pulsates with life.
Populated with plants it is
the world in a bubble —
all we need.

We do not strain to
look beyond the transparent walls
nor remember that glass
is brittle.

We do not notice the
sky outside start to thicken,
turn to steel, descend as though
to crush us.

Are caught unawares by
the thunder's sharp explosion shivering
the fragile structure that
surrounds us.

A hail of silver bullets
strikes the pane above us.
We look up at last
and realise

how thinly screened we are;
how soon our shelter may be shattered,
our world splintered into
smithereens.

On Winning One's Half Century

Wrap up carefully in brown paper;
whitewash all your windows
THEY
used to say,
to save yourself from atom radiation
in an H-bomb war.

Only the other day
omniscient Panorama
poured more whitewash.
In a nuclear affray,
they thoughtfully advised,
do pretty much the same.

And in a way,
watching David Attenborough
on how it all began,
next day,
I reckoned:
we've not changed that much,
we animals of Earth —
we and those molluscs,
mostly now extinct,
who wrapped themselves in shell.
Where are they
today?

I moved house a month or so ago.
And now I'm fifty
have had mortise locks,
spy-holes,
steel meshes,
fitted to my doors and windows.
Yet you bet your life
THEY'LL bust in,
some day.

Fable

Once upon a time
there was something
some people had invented
that could kill everyone
and destroy the whole world.

And I decided
I was someone who could decidc
on behalf of everyone else
whether this should happen.

And I didn't know much
about what this thing was;
but I decided I wanted to be Leader
and decide everything
for everyone else.

So I saw to it that I got appointed.
And in my name I allowed other people,
who knew more about annihilating than I,
to destroy the whole world
and everyone living on it
without consulting them.

This Is Your Death

This is your death
When sunlight breathes on the wall
And you draw the curtain;
When you turn from the ruby-gleam fairground and say,
"Not for me".

This is your death
When the News reports Christ's crucifixion
You lean back and suck your pipe;
When you choose for your nephew's birthday
A miniature megaton rocket.

This is your death
When they lynch a nigger and you answer,
"Progress takes time";
When the tin can drags down the cat's tail
But you cross the road.

This is your death
When the bomber bolts are screwed by your spanner
And you say, "It's only a job";
Or having glimpsed a streak of the morning
You decay into fame.

This is your death
When you state, "I am not me
But two or three people:
A skilled professional slayer
And a kind father".

This is your death
When millions are dying you respond,
"It's up to the others";
When you say, "Life is good"
Yet won't live it —
This, this is your death.

Viewing a Cambodian Casualty

Are you real,
standing among the palms, surrounded by
fellow villagers, photographers
and us?

Your back is pencilled, crinkled, stretched
in a taut unnatural tissue.
You were burned, they say,
four years ago with
scalding jelly from a U.S. bomb.

But are they really scars on flesh
or just a map, a
diagram of human degradation?
Is it skin or paper so
tortured and disfigured?

My eyes glaze.
I merge with the cameras.
My eyes turn to lens.

I no longer see you but
merely a picture with a
horrifying caption.
You are something viewed on the screen;
read about in the papers;
observed at exhibitions.

Jellied petrol may have blistered you, but
I have been chilled by
white hot phosphorous;
my nerves iced;
my glands numbed;
my eyeballs frozen.

I too have been injured.

Jersey Holiday

Jersey (bays and steep-banked lanes,
paddocks where creamy cattle graze,
small vineyards, solid pink stone farms,
old churches, lazy long-stretched strand)

you are no holiday resort — it pours.
We drive through endless maze of streams,
on silver mirrors of the sky,
along the cliff's brink, blurred by rain.

You should be sun-soaked; so should we,
sprawled warm and naked on the shore —
not drenched, chilled, hunched into ourselves,
sheltering separately in our clothes.

And we rain too: showers, cascades;
puddles reflect our shuddering forms.
Rain drops studded on the leaves —
tears fallen from our weeping eyes.

For we are not as we had supposed
linked together, minds entwined.
Water trickles down the rocks;
rain drops spray off into space.

Nor is this island what it seems.
Beneath the pretty pastures — caves.
Bygone barbarism lurks
in deep-ground tunnels, caverns hewn

by broken bloody hands of slaves
labouring under brutal guards,
burrowing bunkers in the depths
of Jersey, underneath the grass.

Then, it was secret chambers carved
by "untermenschen", Poles and Jews;
but now across the narrow sea
deadlier contraptions lie in wait,

all set to exhale nuclear gas,
poison the people, wither fields,
blacken hedgerows, kill the cows —
we realise it is time to leave.

Suddenly the deluge stops.
(Bunker slaves went long ago.)
People rise to quell the fumes.
We are together, free. We stay.

Shock

Rifle butts
plunge into the gut of sleep.
Winded lung
rasps with a whooping choke of
truncheons, triggers, bayonets, canisters,
wheels, chains, propellers.
Black diesel rage of vomit
poured astoundingly into the gasping
belly void of night.

Crack on the skull.
Kick in the groin.
Blow in the abdomen.

Prague. Chicago. Chipraguo.

Only yesterday
we saw a faint film of light
play over the Prairie,
waver across the Steppes;
a pale dawn on
the White Sea,
the Great Lakes:
breath mist on a sheen of glass—
but smashed now to
splintered darkness.

Laughter

Scooter raised wind sweeps the hair,
rushes through its sticky tangles,
dries off stale sweat in the armpits,
blows coat and collar free.

Sun shaft bursts through thunder clouds,
punctures their bulbous bellies,
crashes on the clotted ocean,
shatters it to glittering fragments.

Match flame touches detritus —
a conurbation's dustbin debris,
shrivels curls and blazes up
in a pyramid of fire.

One day in the fetid boardroom
someone opened all the windows;
workers in a weapons plant
used the gunpowder for squibs.
At sermon time on Sunday morning
everybody roared with laughter.

MEMO

From Pat Arrowsmith

To Fellow Amnesty International Workers

Crushed in crammed cabinet,
filed away,
you are stifled,
bones ground to powder.

Every key touch
shocks you,
jumps muscles,
leaps heart-beat,
scorches scrotum,
anus,
nipples.

My biro point
stabs your stomach,
punctures breast,
buttocks,
abdomen;

drafting letters to
prime ministers,
prison governors,
it bleeds,
exudes excrement of terror.

We photostat;
snip news items;
staple case-papers -
and you are flattened,
knifed,
chain-ganged.

Stringing parcels
(records of your agony),
we tighten the noose,
squeeze your throat,
garotte you.

Seated in conclave
we deliberate how to help yo
while you are asphyxiated,
submerged,
drowned.

But is it you,
so certain of your stand,
who is being tortured,
liquidated?

Or we,
thrashed,
electrocuted,
strangled,
time and again;

debating,
recounting,
reporting,
time and again:

writing it up,
making complaints,
filing it away,
time and again -

is it we
who are dying?

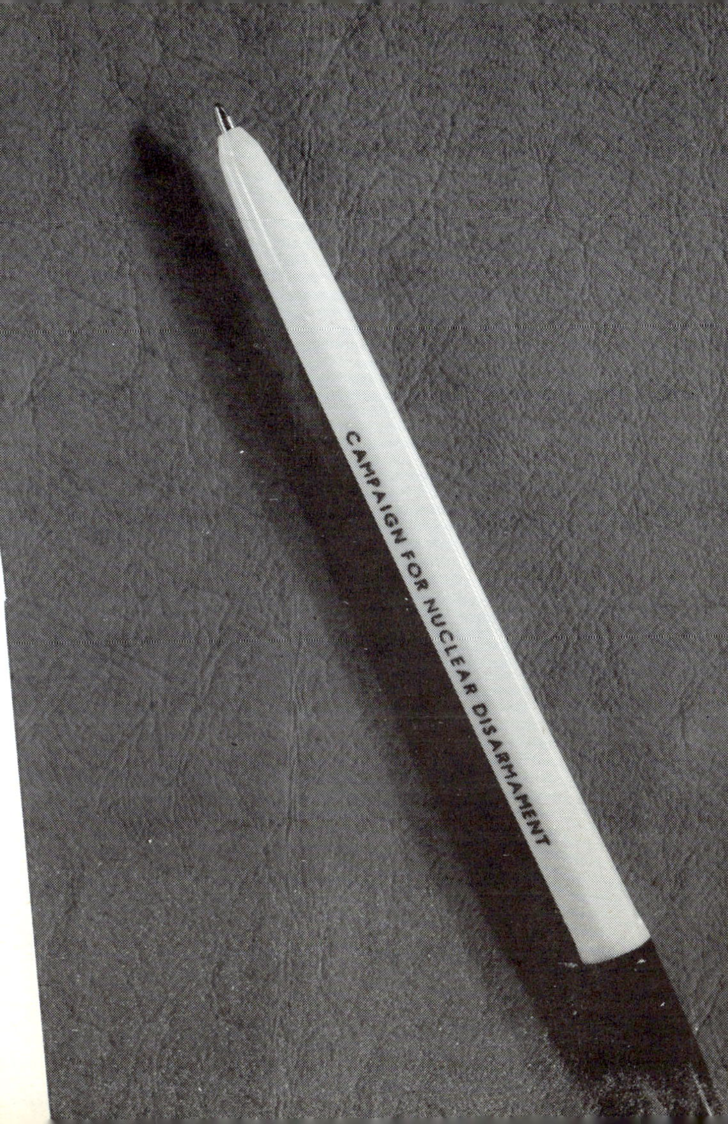

View from Orford Castle

High through the summer afternoon we climb,
sandals flapping on each tread-worn stair,
up the steep tower, sky-scraper of bygone time,
from whose summit we stand and stare

over a landscape only to be seen
in children's story books — a fairy tale
of tiny cattle set in vivid green,
on the distant channel a minute sail.

Toy farmhouses' red roofs are bright
as city tiles never are in real life.
Drugged by the magic sun-filled light
we forget the ancient history of strife:

of bodies gouged and gushing streams of blood,
arrow agony piercing to the bone,
blistered flesh scalded scarlet by the flood
of boiling oil, massive groan

of suffering and slaughter this fortress represents.
It was all so long ago, we say,
historic, even picturesque; such events
can have no bearing on our lives today.

Then miles away across the hedge-stitched land
toyworld ends for ever. On the rim
of vision by the far off strand
we see, hazy in the heat, yet grim

pale greyish khaki humps,
queer, squat, unexplained;
small grubby finger smudges, lumps.
The sunny afternoon is stained

with anger at this ugliness, and sudden fear.
We guess, we almost know those mounds are filled
with deadly gadgets that could tear
the earth to bits; pile those killed

by atom rockets from these modern forts
mountain high; scorch every living thing.
We squint, strive to block off such thoughts,
continue to enjoy the view and cling

to our holiday mood — in vain:
the ruined castle ceases to be quaint;
people are brutal, inhumane
as ever in the past. A taint

of strontium poison permeates the air.
Off in the further reaches of the sky
faint thunder rumbles, clouds appear.
This frail summer's day is going to die.

Cliff City

Climb the last rise.
stand shocked still and stare at
this sudden headland city.

Watch divers glide through the spring sky,
swoop, join the multitude
assembled on the precipice.

Black, white, rank on rank
they stand, sit in their rock streets,
cluster by their dwellings,
jostling each other,
mingling their many timbred voices
into the faint babel of a far-off crowd —
cries of children in a distant playground.

Some take off, leave the city,
tour about, return.
A fierce battle bursts out overhead.
Slight stench rises from the population's detritus.

But the air fight's debris is a frisk of feathers;
the smell, from fish-tanged droppings whitening the cliff;
the streets, a honeycomb of carved out nooks and ledges;
the dwellings, little mounds of seaweed.

For this is not just land's end —
it is world's end.
Here tribes of birds hold sway —
humans count for nothing.
This craggy corner of the Earth belongs to
gannets, gulls, guillemots.
And at its entrance
a menacing great skua stands on guard.

Micro-chip Miscalculation

Granule of military might,
mischievous molecule comprising
million megatonne micro-mind:
omniscient atom brain
suddenly last week got muddled,
made a monstrous minute error,
all-but split and split and split again . . .
in a brilliant flash so searing,
massive earthquake roar so thundering
our globe would have exploded, shrivelled
like a pin pricked toy balloon.

Steel Plant

Lunge through the clotted atmosphere.
Gulp into the furnace of your coke-filled crank-wracked
Belly funnels-full of oxygen to quicken your
Insatiably raging arteries.
Fart it out to choke the lungs of the world with
A stench of spent industrial energy.
For you are what we swear by,
With your blood torrent of liquid force,
Your virility bristling and bursting in clouds densely brilliant
As Guy Fawkes sulphur stars.
In your cavities molten floods are refined by heat purifyingly
Translucent as sun-down on a tropical ocean;
And pincer-wise your mammoth fingers dextrously pick
Immense cubes of blazing metal to place between massive
Molars that spew them forth lean and lashing as serpents' tongues.

Peering through foggy lens at your blinding omnipotence we
Cower at a distance deferentially tidying the chaos of your passage,
And wonder how long the cellophane walls of our
Control cabins can withstand your rage until they crinkle and melt and
Pour into the torrent;
Whose lungs will stay unshrivelled to inhale the suppurating
Death-sigh of your aftermath;
Whose hands remain to sweep away the debris.

Rock Pool

Through film of glass I stare down at an undiscovered planet:
jewel star ringed with silver, set in jet rock shade—
the stone shore glitters with a galaxy of pools.

Below me, just a finger-touch away,
this new world spreads in miniature:
highways in veins of sand and fine-grained shingle;
metropolis of pebbles;
dark gleaming domes of sea anemone;
minarets, pagodas built of shell;
marquees of delicately fluted limpet.
Encircling this a filigree of forest.
Layer on layer of many coloured branch-fronds interweave,
cascade in lemon tendrils,
emerald, sherry-brown.

The rock face rainbows down a wealth of strata:
white turns to barnacle-carved beige;
pink, slate, russet merge in umber;
all watered over, dimmed by palest wash of jade.

Tiny boulders rising from the pool bed grow to mountain ranges.
Pores yawn into caverns.
Dents become crevasses.
Cracks, fissures stretch, expand into deep canyons —
huge gorges through the Himalayas.

There are no people here;
only the fragile sculpture of small crabs;
cellophane flick of shrimps that vanish as you see them.
There is no excrement or garbage;
no silted rivers, strontium or diesel fumes.

Man on the Moon

Speck of an electron,
pin-point flea
hopped a micro-millimetre from one
grain of sand to another
on the vast shore.

Man was on the moon.

He took with him a
tiny dart tipped with
nuclear poison,
stepped out of his capsule,
took aim,
and shot the Man In The Moon
dead.

Sailing to Belfast to Attack the War

The night sky slowly brightens to deep blue.
We stand on deck scarf-huddled in the wind
that hammers us head-on — a threat, a warning
to turn about and sail at once for home.

Our hair streams backward towards Britain,
away from this strange terrifying land
where death snipes from a hidden roof-top,
explodes in blasted buildings, shattered limbs.

But it is early still — the town is quiet.
We talk softly of what lies ahead.
Only the slight engine swish, all else is silent
as the ship knifes smoothly along Belfast Lough

past lighthouses and red or green lamped beacons,
meccano of illuminated cranes and masts,
flare of furnaces, awakening shipyards
brightly stencilled on the still dark dawn.

That was long ago, and we arrived;
did what we had crossed the sea to do;
not shot or gassed or blown to bits, survived,
and boarded ship that night and went back home.

But that voyage through the dawn is not yet over.
I'm on deck now and sliding up the Lough.
Yes, even while I'm in this English prison
I'm still aboard and sailing to Belfast.

The Day the 30 Years' War Ended

And in the end it was all nonsense.
They came for their tin and their tungsten,
their off-shore oil:
ingredients of a greedy, savage society,
to be defended at all costs,
even at the cost of 56 thousand of their own people,
never mind tonnage upon tonnage of dispensable brown flesh.

They came as rich men from the beginning of history have come
to tell poorer, happier people in other countries
how to run their lives.

They came with dagger-bullets,
liquid fire,
clouds of poison,
mammoth block-busters.
They blighted the crops,
withered forests,
burnt the people,
even turned sunshine into rain storms.

All in the name of Freedom and Democracy
they paid the wages of a million police thugs;
poured money into the pockets of vicious puppets;
turned children into prostitutes;
littered quiet market towns with
sleezy bars and massage parlours;
supplied corrupt politicians with instruments of torture
to help them defend Freedom and Democracy
on their behalf.

They came to shore up the ramparts
of their own overfed society;
to prime the purses of the privileged few
who appropriate the wealth of their own country;
to plunder another land
so that their own filth-belching factories and
horrendous war machine kept running.

But in the end they couldn't do it.
People determined to be free
cannot be pillaged and suppressed for ever.
So they were forced at last to leave,
in an absurd fluster of distraught ambassadors,
a chaos of disintegrating chopper blades.

After Wethersfield

Crickets in the grass creak in unison,
Sprung by braced legs blade-high in the air.
They think they are invincible: taut limbs propel them
To the limits of the sky;

Not realising that twig-brittle
Their legs might break, trapped by one plant-frond;
Their rows of prison match-box homes
Splinter at an infant's finger-touch.

In the centrifugal fury of the universe
This bubble world spins on a slender axle
The slightest breath can snap and burst
Into a million smithereens.

Yet wafer-tense their wings continue
To cleave the air and generate a gale.
The vortex of their fragile raging blades
Scythes the path of their own doom;

Until some afternoon emerge
From the strained engine's choking rattle,
The gibberish of the cricket swarm,
Several clearly voiced pronouncements.

Then do you see them
Squarely ranked upon the ground
Face the intricate propellers' flurry,
The galaxy of feckless insects.

For sculptured separately in plastic stone
They are united by a white hot wire
Which draws the insects' frenzied stinging
And cuts through the propeller blades.

Nightfall Through a Plate Glass Window

You might have thought
when my mother died
and the film broke,
reel stopped,
childhood ended,
it would have been
a private loss.

That evening,
sky darkening,
I watched nightfall
on the bay
through a plate glass window.

I saw the room
totally reflected,
bay obliterated,
just the room I was in,
coastline, horizon
almost gone.

Someone saw the badge
that I was wearing.
Twelve men, he said,
had been irradiated
at an atom plant —
damaged, like my mother.

Through the window
mirroring the private room;
through my private loss
sailed a lit-up ship
full of living people,
all irradiated.

I left the room;
left my mother's bedside;
left my childhood;
and went to tell others
what I had seen.

Notes

1 Pat's opposition to British troops being in Northern Ireland stems from her pacifism but is not CND policy.

2 Water colour painting (1966) of a greenhouse where I worked as a Camden Borough gardener.

3 **Greenhouse.** Written summer 1968. Published in *Tribune* and *Doves for the Seventies* (Corgi anthology of peace poems).

4 From the government publication *Protect* (sic) *and Survive*.
On Winning One's Half Century. Written on the eve of going on an anti-cruise missile demonstration (15th March 1980). Published in *Tribune*.

5 **Fable**. 7th July 1980 — after watching a television programme about the impending U.S. presidential election. Published in *Socialist Challenge*.
This is Your Death. Written summer 1962. Published in *Tribune*.

7 **Viewing a Cambodian Casualty.** 9th July 1968. Published in *Help* and *Road Apple Review* (a U.S. magazine). About a young girl I saw on a peace mission to Cambodia in 1968. Her back was so scarred from napalm burns that she looked like a Hiroshima victim.

8 **Jersey Holiday**. Written 1977. Published in *Voices* and *Sappho*. Jersey is riddled with Nazi underground bunkers from World War II and is very close to a French nuclear power plant called Cap Le Hague.

9 **Shock**. Written during the last week of August 1968 when the Warsaw Pact countries were invading Czechoslovakia and the Democratic Presidential Campaign Convention was taking place in Chicago. One of the contestants, Eugene McCarthy, from the Middle West, was opposing the U.S. war in Vietnam. Published in *Sanity* and *Ambience*.
Laughter. Written summer 1969. Published in *Sanity*.

10 **Memo**. 25th October 1976. Published in *New Poetry*.

12 Hiroshima, August 1945, looking north-west from 'ground zero'.

13 **View from Orford Castle**. Written in 1975 during the week of the 30th anniversary of Hiroshima Day. Published in *Sanity* and *Peace News*.

14 **Cliff City.** 11th July 1973. Published in *Birds*.
Micro-chip Miscalculation. 12th June 1980. Published in *Socialist Challenge*. This poem was a response to the news that nuclear war had twice nearly broken out by mistake as the result of a 'technical error'.

15 **Steel Plant**. 9th March 1956. Published in *Expression*.

16 Water colour studies of rock pools on a beach in Ireland, 1966.

17 **Rock Pool**. 1st February 1970. Published in *Expression*.

18 **Man on the Moon**. Written on 21st July 1969 in eight minutes flat after hearing the news that 'man' had landed on the moon. Published in *Tribune*.
Sailing to Belfast to Attack the War. 1974. On New Year's Day 1972, 'Irish Action', an English peace group, sailed to Belfast to leaflet British troops there. This poem was written over two years later when I was in Holloway Prison for again leafleting soldiers — this time in England — about the war. Published in *Tribune* and *Breakout*.

19 **The Day the 30 Years' War Ended**. May 1975. Written on the day the Vietnam War ended. Published in *Tribune*.

20 **After Wethersfield**. Written in January 1962 when I was in Holloway Prison after taking part in non-violent resistance organised by the peace movement at the Wethersfield USAF H-bomber base. Published in *Tribune* and *Breakout*.
'You Profess Peace. We Practise It' — Non-violent resistance at a nuclear weapons base, December 1961.

21 **Nightfall Through a Plate Glass Window**. Published in *Tribune*. Written on 21st September 1978, the day my mother died. I was in a hotel in Torquay where a man saw my CND badge and told me about an accident at Hinkley Point nuclear power station nearby. I immediately went and rang up the press.

24 **Violence**. Water colours. 1955. Silver and gold hands on Indian ink background. Red hands in green bubble at centre.